Boots COOKSHOP
— FOOD —
PROCESSOR
COOKBOOK

COOKSHOP

— FOOD —

PROCESSOR

COOKBOOK

Cover photograph by Chris Crofton
Inside photography by John Lee

Published on behalf of
The Boots Company plc, Nottingham
by Hamlyn Publishing,
a division of The Hamlyn Publishing Group Ltd,
Bridge House, London Road, Twickenham,
Middlesex, England

First published under the title
Kitchen Magic

ISBN 0 600 32554 7

Set in Gill Sans
by Photocomp Ltd, Birmingham

Printed in Italy

Contents

Useful Facts & Figures

Notes on metrication

In this book quantities are given in metric and Imperial measures. Exact conversion from Imperial to metric measures does not usually give very convenient working quantities and so the metric measures have been rounded off into units of 25 grams. The table below shows the recommended equivalents.

Ounces	Approx g to nearest whole figure	Recommended conversion to nearest unit of 25
1	28	25
2	57	50
3	85	75
4	113	100
5	142	150
6	170	175
7	198	200
8	227	225
9	255	250
10	283	275
11	312	300
12	340	350
13	368	375
14	396	400
15	425	425
16 (1 lb)	454	450
17	482	475
18	510	500
19	539	550
20 (1¼ lb)	567	575

Note When converting quantities over 20 oz first add the appropriate figures in the centre column, then adjust to the nearest unit of 25. As a general guide, 1 kg (1000 g) equals 2·2 lb or about 2 lb 3 oz. This method of conversion gives good results in nearly all cases, although in certain pastry and cake recipes a more accurate conversion is necessary to produce a balanced recipe.

Liquid measures The millilitre has been used in this book and the following table gives a few examples.

Imperial	Approx ml to nearest whole figure	Recommended ml
¼ pint	142	150 ml
½ pint	283	300 ml
¾ pint	425	450 ml
1 pint	567	600 ml
1½ pints	851	900 ml
1¾ pints	992	1000 ml (1 litre)

Spoon measures All spoon measures given in this book are level unless otherwise stated.

Can sizes At present, cans are marked with the exact (usually to the nearest whole number) metric equivalent of the Imperial weight of the contents, so we have followed this practice when giving can sizes.

Oven temperatures

The table below gives recommended equivalents.

	°C	°F	Gas
Very cool	110	225	¼
	120	250	½
Cool	140	275	1
	150	300	2
Moderate	160	325	3
	180	350	4
Moderately hot	190	375	5
	200	400	6
Hot	220	425	7
	230	450	8
Very hot	240	475	9

Note *When making any of the recipes in this book, only follow one set of measures as they are not interchangeable.*

Introduction

All About Food Processors

The food processor must surely be one of the most efficient machines to come on the market in recent years. Whether you are a housewife, have a full-time job and a family to cater for, prepare dishes in bulk for the freezer, or simply enjoy entertaining, the food processor can help you. It takes all the tedious labour and time out of preparing both raw and cooked foods in any recipe.

There are several brands of food processor on the market, each having the same basic design and attachments. They are extremely versatile and can chop, grate, mince, slice, purée, beat or knead, literally in seconds. Certain machines are also designed to aerate mixtures – for example, whisking egg whites – but this is not a standard feature. The different types of machine have different attachments for mixing, chopping, slicing, grating or making chips.

How to use your Food Processor

1 Always read the manufacturer's instructions carefully before use.
2 Never overload the machine, as this will strain the motor. It is far better to prepare small batches of food.
3 The bowl is able to withstand boiling liquid, but this could splash dangerously, so allow liquids to cool slightly before adding them to the bowl.
4 Always let the blades stop moving before removing the lid.
5 Handle the blades carefully as they are sharp, and keep out of the reach of children.
6 Make sure the bowl or container is firmly in position before fitting any attachments, and before switching on the machine.
7 Always use the plastic pusher when grating or slicing food – never push with your fingers.
8 Check that you have the correct attachment fitted before putting any food in the bowl.
9 When adding liquids to other ingredients, pour through the feed tube while the machine is running.
10 When you first use the machine, keep an eye on the ingredients you are processing, remembering that the machine works very fast.

Care of your Food Processor

Do not immerse the motor base in water, simply wipe clean using a damp cloth. Wash the bowl or container and all the attachments in hot soapy water and rinse well (these can also go in a dishwasher). Take care when drying to avoid touching the sharp blades.

The attachments and their uses

The double-bladed chopping knife
This metal chopping blade is probably the most versatile of all attachments, enabling you to chop, mix, beat, purée, mince, make breadcrumbs, pastry, bread and much more. However, care must be taken not to overchop food – a few seconds too long could mean the difference between a chopped onion and a purée!

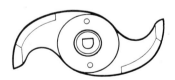

Chopping: Always cut the food into even-sized pieces before chopping in the machine, otherwise the food will be unevenly prepared. If the food is particularly hard, drop it through the feed tube on to the revolving blades, if the machine has this facility. If in any one recipe, there are several foods to be chopped, make sure that you do not overchop at the beginning before adding the remaining ingredients.

The recipes in this book have been written so that the ingredients are chopped in the correct order to prevent having to wash up between processes.

When chopping herbs or making breadcrumbs, make sure the bowl and the herbs are completely dry, otherwise you could end up with a soggy mess!

Plastic mixing blade

Mixing: This process is carried out using the double-bladed chopping knife or the plastic mixing blade if the machine has one. It is important not to overprocess food and result in puréeing or liquidising instead of mixing. Cake mixtures, dips and pastries are made in this way. The food processor is particularly useful for preparing one-stage cake mixtures.

Puréeing: This process is carried out using the double-bladed chopping knife. It is ideal for making batters, baby foods, sauces, soups, pâtés, fruit and vegetable purées and for invalid dishes. It is important to check the quantity of food that the bowl will hold.

Mincing or grinding: The machine is invaluable for this, whether you want to mince raw or cooked food. Always make sure that the food is cut up evenly before putting into the machine, otherwise it will be unevenly processed.

Slicing and shredding attachments
A range of slicing and grating discs are available to fit on to the central spindle in the plastic bowl. In most machines the food is placed in the feed tube and pushed on to the revolving disc, using the plastic pusher as a guide. The more pressure you apply, the thicker the slice. The sliced food is

collected in the plastic bowl, which is emptied as necessary. If necessary, cut the food to fit into the feed tube. Attachments are available to cut a variety of different thicknesses of slices, to grate particularly difficult foods, such as Parmesan cheese, and to convert the food processor into a juice extractor.

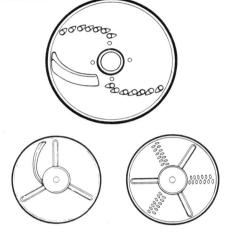

Slicing or shredding and grating discs

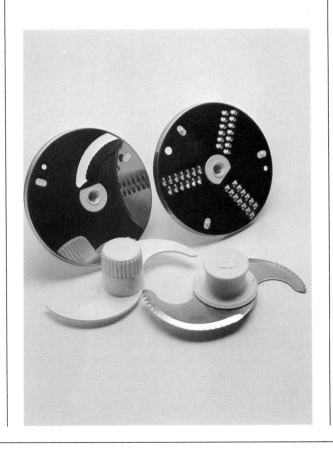

Soups & Starters

When it comes to preparing chunky soups or the first course of the meal, the food processor really does play a leading role. No more laborious chopping or slicing of vegetables or sieving.

Using a food processor to make terrines and pâtés of all types saves hours compared to traditional methods of mincing the ingredients several times. If the pâté is a smooth one, you will find that using your food processor produces a result far smoother than by old-fashioned methods. The same ease of preparation is evident when preparing creamy savoury mousses and soufflés or pastry-based starters. Owning a food processor really does mean that you can prepare a simple or sophisticated starter in minutes.

SMOKED HADDOCK SOUP

SERVES 4

100 g/4 oz potato
½ medium onion
225 g/8 oz smoked haddock
grated rind and juice of ½ lemon
25 g/1 oz butter
25 g/1 oz plain flour
600 ml/1 pint vegetable stock
300 ml/½ pint milk
pinch of dried tarragon
1 teaspoon dried basil
¼ teaspoon turmeric
salt and freshly ground black pepper
few sprigs parsley to garnish

Peel and quarter the potato and onion, and cut the raw fish into 2·5-cm/1–in cubes. Place these ingredients in the bowl and chop finely, using the double-bladed chopping knife. Add the grated lemon rind and mix well.

Melt the butter and fry the chopped ingredients for a few minutes. Stir in the flour and add the stock, milk, dried herbs, turmeric and salt and pepper to taste.

Bring this to the boil, stirring continuously, and simmer for 30 minutes. Stir in the lemon juice and serve hot, garnished with parsley.

CRÈME DE POISSON

SERVES 6

3 leeks
2 medium potatoes
1·15 litres/2 pints stock
salt
1 (227-g/8-oz) can tomatoes
225 g/8 oz cod
few sprigs parsley
300 ml/½ pint milk
freshly ground black pepper
pinch of celery salt
150 ml/¼ pint single cream

Clean the leeks and stand them vertically in the feed tube. Slice, using the slicing disc. Repeat this with the potatoes. Place the sliced vegetables in a saucepan with the stock and salt. Bring to the boil and simmer for 5-8 minutes. Add the tomatoes, cod and parsley and cook for a further 5 minutes. Allow to cool slightly then purée until smooth, using the double-bladed chopping knife. Stir in the milk, pepper and celery salt. Reheat and add the cream just before serving.

TOMATO AND CARROT SOUP

SERVES 4 - 6

1 small onion
175 g/6 oz carrots
450 g/1 lb tomatoes
50 g/2 oz butter
50 g/2 oz plain flour
1·15 litres/2 pints mixed herb stock,
made with a stock cube
1 teaspoon castor sugar
1 teaspoon dried oregano
½ teaspoon paprika
½ teaspoon ground mace
2 tablespoons concentrated tomato purée
salt and freshly ground black pepper
6 tablespoons single cream

Peel and roughly slice the onion and carrots; peel and slice the tomatoes.

Place the onion and carrots in the bowl and chop roughly, using the double-bladed chopping knife. Add the sliced tomatoes and continue until the mixture is finely chopped.

Melt the butter in a saucepan and lightly sauté the chopped vegetables. Stir in the flour and add the stock, sugar, oregano, spices, tomato purée and seasonings. Bring to the boil and simmer gently for 30 minutes.

Pour the soup into the bowl and purée until smooth, using the double-bladed chopping knife. Reheat and serve hot in individual bowls with a tablespoon of single cream swirled on top of each.

Variation

Tomato and Orange Soup Omit the carrots from the above recipe and add 1 medium potato, preparing it in the same way as the carrots. Double the quantity of tomatoes and add the grated rind and juice of 1 large orange to the puréed soup before it is reheated.

To Peel Tomatoes Place the tomatoes in a bowl and pour in freshly boiling water. Leave for 30-60 seconds (depending on the ripeness of the fruit), then drain the fruit. Make a small slit in the tomato peel and the rest should slide off easily.

CREAM OF FENNEL SOUP

SERVES 4

2 heads of fennel, about 575 g/1 ¼ lb
juice of ½ lemon
40 g/1 ½ oz butter
40 g/1 ½ oz plain flour
600 ml/1 pint chicken stock, made
with a stock cube
300 ml/½ pint milk
½ teaspoon ground mace
salt and freshly ground black pepper
few sprigs parsley

Trim and wash the fennel. Cut into quarters and cook in boiling salted water with the lemon juice until tender – about 30 minutes.

Drain the fennel and slice roughly. Melt the butter in a large saucepan and sauté the fennel for a few minutes. Stir in the flour, then add half the stock and milk, the ground mace and seasoning.

Finely chop the parsley, using the double-bladed chopping knife. Place the fennel and stock mixture in the bowl with the parsley and purée until smooth, using the double-bladed chopping knife. Return this mixture to the saucepan, add the remaining stock and milk and bring to the boil. Simmer gently, stirring occasionally for 10-15 minutes. Serve hot, garnished with a sprig of fennel.

Variation

Cream of Celery Soup Substitute 1 small head of celery for the fennel in the above recipe. Trim and reserve some of the leaves for garnish. Separate the sticks of celery and slice them using the slicing disc. Continue as in the main recipe.

From the top: Cream of Fennel Soup, French Onion Soup (overleaf) and Tomato and Carrot Soup

FRENCH ONION SOUP
SERVES 4

450 g/1 lb onions
50 g/2 oz butter
1 tablespoon oil
few sprigs parsley
900 ml/1 ½ pints beef stock, made with
2 stock cubes
1 teaspoon yeast extract
salt and freshly ground black pepper
To serve:
½ French loaf
175 g/6 oz Gruyère cheese

Peel and halve the onions. Fit the slicing disc and feed the onions into the bowl to slice them.

Melt the butter and oil in a pan. Add the sliced onion and stir well. Leave over a low heat to brown.

Finely chop the parsley, using the double-bladed chopping knife.

Add the stock, yeast extract and parsley to the onion. Season to taste. Simmer the soup for 20 minutes.

For the topping, cut the French bread into slices and toast each slice on one side only. Cut the cheese so that it will fit into the feed tube, then grate it using the grating disc. When the soup has almost finished cooking, pile the cheese on the untoasted side of the bread slices and cook under the grill until lightly browned. Pour the soup into individual bowls and top each portion with the cheese on bread. Serve immediately.

BEETROOT AND ORANGE SOUP
SERVES 4

450 g/1 lb cooked beetroot
1 (178-g/6¼-fl oz) can concentrated orange juice
salt and freshly ground black pepper
4 tablespoons whipping cream
grated rind of ½ orange

Peel and halve the beetroot, then chop finely using the double-bladed chopping knife. Make up the orange juice according to the instructions on the can. Gradually add to the beetroot through the feed tube and purée until the mixture is smooth.

Pour the soup into a bowl, season to taste and chill in the refrigerator.

Whip the cream lightly in a small bowl and fold in the grated orange rind.

Stir the soup and serve in individual bowls with a tablespoon of cream floating on each.

Note Rinse the bowl and double-bladed chopping knife as soon as the beetroot mixture is removed, to avoid staining.

CUCUMBER GAZPACHO

SERVES 4

1 small onion
few sprigs parsley
1 sprig mint
1 clove garlic
1 cucumber
1 teaspoon lemon juice
½ teaspoon Worcestershire sauce
1 teaspoon wine vinegar
600 ml/1 pint tomato juice
salt and freshly ground black pepper
Garnish:
ice cubes · croûtons

Peel and quarter the onion. Place it with the parsley, mint and garlic in the bowl and chop finely, using the double-bladed chopping knife.

Peel the cucumber and cut into 5-cm/2-in lengths. Feed into the bowl until roughly chopped. Mix with the remaining ingredients and chill well. Float ice cubes or croûtons on top.

CREAM OF CUCUMBER SOUP

SERVES 4

1 onion
25 g/1 oz butter
25 g/1 oz plain flour
300 ml/½ pint chicken stock
1 cucumber
450 ml/¾ pint milk
salt and freshly ground black pepper
freshly grated nutmeg
pinch of cayenne
150 ml/¼ pint single cream
few sprigs parsley
a few cucumber slices to garnish (optional)

Peel and quarter the onion. Chop finely, using the double-bladed chopping knife.

Melt the butter and sauté the onion until soft but not browned. Stir in the flour and cook for 1 minute. Stir in the stock and bring to the boil, stirring all the time.

Peel the cucumber and chop roughly, using the double-bladed chopping knife. Stir the cucumber into the soup with the milk, seasoning, nutmeg and cayenne, and simmer for 5–10 minutes. Cool slightly then purée until smooth. Chop the parsley using the double-bladed chopping knife.

Chill the soup thoroughly then stir in the cream and parsley just before serving. Garnish with cucumber slices if you like.

Accompaniments to serve with soup

Croûtons To make croûtons, cut the crusts off medium-thick slices of bread, then cut the bread into small, evenly sized cubes. Fry these in a mixture of butter and oil, turning the cubes frequently until golden brown and crisp. Drain on absorbent kitchen paper before serving with the soup. The croûtons can be flavoured with chopped fresh herbs or garlic.

Crispy Bacon Lean streaky bacon, rind removed, can be cut into small pieces, then fried until crisp. Drain on absorbent kitchen paper and serve with the soup.

Cream of Cucumber Soup

SMOKED HADDOCK PÂTÉ

SERVES 6

450 g/1lb smoked haddock
175 g/6 oz cream cheese
75 g/3 oz butter, melted
grated rind of ½ lemon
1 tablespoon lemon juice
freshly ground black pepper
1 clove garlic, crushed
Garnish:
wedges of lemon
1 bay leaf

Poach the haddock gently in a little water for about 10-15 minutes, until cooked. Drain, cool, remove the skin and flake the fish.

Place the flaked fish in the bowl with the cream cheese and melted butter and blend until smooth, using the double-bladed chopping knife. Add the remaining ingredients and continue to blend until the mixture is smooth. Turn the mixture into a serving dish, or six individual ramekins, chill and serve garnished with wedges of lemon and a bay leaf.

COD'S ROE PÂTÉ

SERVES 4 - 6

¼ onion
1 slice white bread, crusts removed
2 (100-g/3½-oz) cans cod's roe
1 medium potato, boiled
1 clove garlic, crushed
few sprigs parsley
juice of ½ lemon
1 teaspoon oil
salt and freshly ground black pepper
Garnish:
4-6 lettuce leaves
black olives
slices of lemon

Grate the onion using the grating disc. Place the bread and cod's roe in the bowl and, using the double-bladed chopping knife, mix until well blended. Add the potato, garlic and parsley and continue blending until smooth. Add the onion to the mixture together with the lemon juice, oil and seasoning. Blend until smooth. Chill.

Place a lettuce leaf on individual plates, and spoon the pâté on top. Garnish with black olives and slices of lemon. Serve with fingers of toast.

PORK AND SPINACH TERRINE

SERVES 4 - 6

450 g/1 lb lean boneless pork
1 onion
1 clove garlic
50 g/2 oz streaky bacon, rinds removed
1 slice white bread, crusts removed
few sprigs fresh sage
few sprigs parsley
beaten egg to mix
100 g/4 oz frozen leaf spinach, defrosted
salt and freshly ground black pepper
150 ml/¼ pint aspic jelly
Garnish:
slice of orange
bay leaves
few juniper berries

Finely chop the pork, using the double-bladed chopping knife. Peel and quarter the onion then chop with the garlic and bacon. Add to the pork. Make breadcrumbs using the double-bladed chopping knife.

Again using the double-bladed chopping knife, coarsely chop the herbs and stir into the meat. Add sufficient beaten egg to give a soft mixture.

Finely chop the spinach, using the double-bladed chopping knife and season well.

Place half the meat mixture in a 1-litre/1½-pint ovenproof terrine, then add the chopped spinach and finish with the remaining meat, packing it down well. Cover and place the terrine in a baking tin, half filled with water. Bake in a moderate oven (180 C, 350 F, gas 4) for 1¼-1½ hours. Allow to cool.

Pour the aspic jelly over the top of the terrine. Garnish with the slice of orange, bay leaves and a few juniper berries and leave until set.

Note Serve the terrine with warmed French bread, hot toast or melba toast (very thin crisp toast). Crisp celery sticks or radishes can also be served to complement the terrine.

POTTED MEAT PÂTÉ

S E R V E S 4 - 6

225 g/8 oz belly pork
225 g/8 oz veal
100 g/4 oz chicken livers
100 g/4 oz streaky bacon, rinds removed
1 clove garlic
few sprigs parsley
10 juniper berries
¼ teaspoon mustard seed
freshly grated nutmeg
salt and freshly ground black pepper
grated rind of ½ lemon
1 tablespoon brandy
1 tablespoon red wine

Using the double-bladed chopping knife, finely chop the pork, veal, chicken livers, bacon, garlic and parsley. Crush the juniper berries and mustard seed in a pestle and mortar or with a rolling pin.

Mix all the ingredients together and place in a greased 600-ml/1-pint soufflé dish. Cover with foil and stand in a baking tin two-thirds filled with water. Bake in a moderate oven (180C, 350F, gas 4) for 1-1¼ hours.

Allow to cool and place weights on top. Chill overnight.

WELSH LEEK FLAN

S E R V E S 4 - 6

225 g/8 oz cheese pastry
(see page 63)
3 leeks
25 g/1 oz butter
50 g/2 oz ham
2 eggs
150 ml/¼ pint single cream
freshly grated nutmeg
salt and freshly ground black pepper
few sprigs parsley
75 g/3 oz Gruyère cheese

Make the pastry and use to line a 20-cm/8-in flan ring. Bake blind in a moderately hot oven (200C, 400F, gas 6) for 15 minutes.

Clean the leeks and slice, using the slicing disc. Sauté them in the butter for 5 minutes. Chop the ham finely, using the double-bladed chopping knife, then add the eggs, cream, nutmeg, seasoning and parsley and mix together thoroughly.

Place the leeks in the base of the flan and pour in the egg mixture.

Grate the cheese, using the grating disc, then sprinkle over the flan. Bake in a moderately hot oven (190C, 375F, gas 5) for 30-40 minutes.

CHICKEN TERRINE

S E R V E S 6

100 g/4 oz mushrooms
1 onion
2 slices white bread
few sprigs parsley
1 (1·5-kg/3¼-lb) chicken
100 g/4 oz chicken livers
1 tablespoon chopped fresh tarragon
1 egg, beaten
1 tablespoon single cream
1 tablespoon red wine
grated rind of ½ lemon
salt and freshly ground black pepper
7 rashers streaky bacon

Clean the mushrooms and peel and quarter the onion. Place them in the bowl with the bread and parsley and chop finely, using the double-bladed chopping knife. Transfer to a mixing bowl.

Remove the flesh from the chicken and chop finely together with the chicken livers, using the double-bladed chopping knife. Combine this with the breadcrumb mixture and add all the remaining ingredients except the bacon. Stretch the bacon rashers on a board, using the back of a knife. Use the rashers to line a 1-kg/2-lb loaf tin. Turn the chicken mixture into the lined loaf tin and cover the top with foil. Stand this in a baking tin two-thirds filled with water. Bake in a moderate oven (180C, 350F, gas 4) for 1½-2 hours. Allow to cool and chill well before serving.

From the top: Potted Meat Pâté, Moules Provençales (overleaf) and Welsh Leek Flan

Fish & Seafood

Fish is often neglected in our daily diets but with a little imagination and the help of your food processor a host of delicious dishes can be prepared to serve to all the family or for special dinner parties. Processed to make croquettes, prepared with a special stuffing or coated in a delicious sauce — all these ideas and more can be found in this chapter. Why not look through the pages and select a fish dish for your next main meal?

SMOKED HADDOCK MOUSSAKA

SERVES 4

3 aubergines
2 small onions
4 tablespoons oil
1 (425-g/15-oz) can tomatoes
salt and freshly ground black pepper
1 tablespoon chopped parsley
pinch of cayenne
450 g/1 lb smoked haddock
2 eggs, beaten
150 ml/¼ pint natural yogurt
Garnish:
chopped parsley
wedges of lemon

Slice the aubergines, sprinkle with salt and leave for 30 minutes. Meanwhile, peel and finely chop the onions, using the double-bladed chopping knife. Sauté in one tablespoon of the oil until soft but not golden..Add the tomatoes, seasoning, parsley and cayenne and cook for 5 minutes. Roughly chop the smoked haddock and stir it into the pan. Cook gently for 5 minutes.

Rinse the aubergines well and drain. Fry them in the remaining oil for about 5 minutes. Layer the fish and aubergines alternately in an ovenproof dish, finishing with a layer of aubergines. Combine the eggs and yogurt and pour over the aubergines. Bake in a moderate oven (180 C, 350 F, gas 4) for 20-25 minutes. Garnish with chopped parsley and wedges of lemon.

MOULES PROVENÇALES

SERVES 4

1·75 litres/3 pints mussels
2 slices white bread, crusts removed
3 spring onions
few sprigs parsley
100 g/4 oz butter
1-2 cloves garlic
salt and freshly ground black pepper
chopped parsley to garnish

Scrub the mussels well, removing the beards and discarding any open shells. Place the mussels in a steamer or a colander standing over a saucepan of boiling water and steam for 3 minutes until the shells are just opening. Discard any that do not open. Remove from the heat and break off the empty half of each shell.

Make breadcrumbs, using the double-bladed chopping knife. Finely chop the onions and parsley, using the double-bladed chopping knife. Add the breadcrumbs and the remaining ingredients and mix well. Spread a little of the mixture over each mussel. Just before serving place the mussels under a hot grill until lightly browned. Garnish with chopped parsley.

FISHERMAN'S SURPRISE

SERVES 4

450 g/1 lb potatoes
salt and freshly ground black pepper
175 g/6 oz frozen cod or hake steaks, defrosted
few sprigs of parsley
2 tablespoons single cream
grated rind of 1 lemon
2 eggs, separated
2 tablespoons natural yogurt

Peel the potatoes and boil until tender. Purée the cooked potatoes until smooth using the double-bladed chopping knife and adding seasoning to taste. Spoon the potato from the bowl into a piping bag fitted with a large vegetable star nozzle and pipe a border round the edge of four greased scallop shells or individual ovenproof dishes.

Cut the defrosted fish steaks into chunks and place in the bowl with the parsley and cream. Add seasoning and the grated lemon rind, then mix using the double-bladed chopping knife.

Divide the mixture between the scallop shells or dishes keeping it neatly within the piped potato.

Mix the egg yolks and yogurt. Whisk the egg whites until stiff and fold into the egg yolk mixture with a metal spoon. Spread this mixture over the fish.

Bake in a moderately hot oven (200 C, 400 F, gas 6) for 20 minutes until cooked through and golden brown on top. Serve hot.

CROQUETTES WITH GREEN MAYONNAISE
SERVES 4

450 g/1 lb mixed fish (shrimps, cod,
smoked haddock), cooked
40 g/1 ½ oz butter
40 g/1 ½ oz plain flour
300 ml/½ pint milk
25 g/1 oz Cheddar cheese, grated
1 egg yolk
2 tablespoons chopped parsley
salt and freshly ground black pepper
beaten egg
75 g/3 oz dry white breadcrumbs
fat for deep frying
To serve:
Green mayonnaise (see page 70)

Remove any skin and bones from the fish and then chop, using the double-bladed chopping knife.

Place the butter, flour and milk in a saucepan and bring to the boil, whisking all the time. Allow to cool slightly then beat in the cheese, egg yolk, parsley, seasoning and fish. Spread the mixture on a plate and chill thoroughly. Divide the mixture into 8 and shape into croquettes. Coat the croquettes with egg and breadcrumbs. Heat the oil to 185 C/360 F or until a cube of day-old bread turns golden. Fry the croquettes for 5-6 minutes and drain well. Serve hot with green mayonnaise and a salad if you like.

Variation
The same mixture can be served as a hot savoury — form the mixture into about 30 small balls and coat each one with beaten egg and breadcrumbs. Fry a few at a time, as above, keeping the cooked ones hot. Serve with the green mayonnaise as a dip.

COD MIMOSA
SERVES 4

3 onions
2 tablespoons oil
675 g/1 ½ lb cod, cooked and flaked
100 g/4 oz split peas, soaked
overnight and cooked
2 tablespoons chopped parsley
2 teaspoons white wine vinegar
1 clove garlic, crushed
salt and freshly ground black pepper
18 black olives
3 hard-boiled eggs
chopped parsley to garnish

Peel and finely chop the onions, using the double-bladed chopping knife. Fry in the oil until soft, but not golden. Stir in the cod and split peas and cook for 2 minutes. Add the parsley, wine vinegar, garlic and seasoning. Cook for a further 2-3 minutes. Place in a serving dish and scatter with olives. Coarsely chop the hard-boiled eggs, using the double-bladed chopping knife. Sprinkle over the fish and garnish with chopped parsley. Serve hot.

Note This is a dish which is particularly popular with children. If preparing this dish for children, remember to remove or reduce the garlic and replace the olives with wedges of tomato.

Croquettes with Green Mayonnaise

PEPPERED BURGERS

SERVES 4

1 onion
1 slice bread
few sprigs parsley
225 g/8 oz braising or chuck steak
2 rashers bacon, rinds removed
salt
1 egg, beaten
1 tablespoon black peppercorns
25 g/1 oz butter
1 tablespoon pure corn oil
To serve:
Spicy tomato sauce (see page 72)

Peel and quarter the onion. Chop the bread, onion and parsley together, using the double-bladed chopping knife. Set aside. Trim the meat and mince together with the bacon, using the double-bladed chopping knife. Return the chopped onion mixture to the bowl and season. Add the beaten egg and mix together. Shape the mixture into four burgers. Crush the peppercorns in a pestle and mortar and press into the burgers.

Heat the butter and oil in a frying pan and fry the burgers for 10-15 minutes, turning once during cooking. Drain well and serve with spicy tomato sauce.

Peppered Burgers

STEAK TARTARE

SERVES 4

1 onion
450 g/1 lb lean beef
5 egg yolks, kept separate
few drops Tabasco sauce
salt and freshly ground black pepper
chopped parsley
To serve:
finely chopped spring onions
chopped capers
chopped anchovies

Peel and quarter the onion and chop finely, using the double-bladed chopping knife. Roughly chop the meat, then chop until coarsely ground, using the double-bladed chopping knife. Mix in the chopped onion, one of the egg yolks, Tabasco sauce and seasoning.

Divide the meat into four patties and place on individual serving plates. Make a depression in the centre of each. Place an egg yolk in each depression and sprinkle with chopped parsley. Serve with small bowls of finely chopped spring onions, capers and anchovies.

GUARD OF HONOUR WITH APRICOT STUFFING

SERVES 6

2 joints best end neck of lamb, chined
4 slices white bread, crusts removed
few sprigs parsley and mint
40 g/1 ½ oz margarine
1 small onion, chopped
75 g/3 oz dried apricots, chopped
salt and freshly ground black pepper
beaten egg to bind

Choose joints of lamb with six or seven chops on each. Trim the bones to within 2·5 cm/1 in of the top. Place the joints together allowing the bones to cross alternately with the bases together. Secure with string.

Place the bread, parsley and mint in the bowl and mix, using the double-bladed chopping knife. Turn the mixture into a mixing bowl. Melt the margarine and sauté the onion. Stir into the breadcrumb mixture with the remaining ingredients, adding egg to bind.

Fill the cavity between the two joints of meat with the stuffing. Cover the end of each bone with foil to prevent burning. Place the meat in a roasting tin and roast in a moderately hot oven (190 C, 375 F, gas 5) for 1 ¼-1 ½ hours. Remove the foil and replace with cutlet frills. Serve with a lightly cooked green vegetable such as broccoli.

Note Apricot stuffing is also delicious with roast pork dishes. Instead of using mint, substitute sprigs of rosemary or sage. Shoulder leg or loin of pork can be filled with this mixture.

STUFFED LAMB CHOPS

SERVES 4

4 loin lamb chops
Stuffing:
2 slices white bread, crusts removed
few sprigs mint
few sprigs rosemary
½ small onion, roughly chopped
grated rind of ½ lemon
beaten egg to bind
salt and freshly ground black pepper
Garnish:
watercress sprigs
quarters of tomato

Slit the chops horizontally through to the bone, to form a pocket.

Place the bread with the remaining ingredients in the bowl and, using the double-bladed chopping knife, blend until a fairly moist stuffing is formed. Divide into four and fill the cavity in each of the chops. Wrap each one in foil. Cook in a moderately hot oven (190 C, 375 F, gas 5) for 20-25 minutes. Unwrap and garnish. Serve with sautéed mushrooms.

Guard of Honour with Apricot Stuffing

GALANTINE OF CHICKEN
S E R V E S   6

1 (1·5-kg/3¼-lb) chicken
1 tablespoon oil for cooking
Stuffing:
1 onion
50 g/2 oz butter
225 g/8 oz ham
100 g/4 oz lean pork
50 g/2 oz walnuts
100 g/4 oz mushrooms
few sprigs fresh tarragon
few sprigs parsley
grated rind of ½ lemon
1 egg, beaten
15 g/½ oz pistachio nuts, blanched and skinned
salt and freshly ground black pepper
Topping:
2 slices white bread
few sprigs parsley
2 tablespoons grated Parmesan cheese
1 clove garlic, crushed

Bone the chicken, taking care not to slit or cut the skin. Lay the boned chicken on a board, skin side downwards.

Peel and quarter the onion and chop finely, using the double-bladed chopping knife. Sauté in half the butter until tender. Finely chop the ham and pork, using the double-bladed chopping knife, and add to the sautéed onion. Coarsely chop the walnuts and mushrooms with the herbs and stir into the meat mixture. Add the remaining ingredients and mix well.

Spread the stuffing over the chicken and shape into a roll, sewing up the edges of the chicken to enclose the stuffing.

To make the topping, make the bread into breadcrumbs, using the double-bladed chopping knife, then add a few sprigs of parsley and chop finely. Stir in the Parmesan cheese and garlic. Spread the remaining butter all over the chicken and then sprinkle with the topping. Place in a baking tin with the tablespoon of oil.

Bake in a moderately hot oven (190 C, 375 F, gas 5) for 1-1½ hours. Serve hot or cold.

PASTA BOLOGNESE
S E R V E S   4 - 6

3 sticks celery
2 carrots
1 onion
1 clove garlic
25 g/1 oz butter
2 tablespoons oil
350 g/12 oz chuck steak
225 g/8 oz lamb's liver
1 (396-g/14-oz) can tomatoes
3 tablespoons red wine
few drops of Tabasco sauce
salt and freshly ground black pepper
3 tablespoons chopped parsley
To serve:
450 g/1 lb tagliatelle or spaghetti
25 g/1 oz butter

Peel or scrape, then finely chop the vegetables and garlic, using the double-bladed chopping knife. Sauté in the butter and oil until soft.

Chop the meat and liver, using the double-bladed chopping knife, and add to the sautéed vegetables. Mix in the remaining ingredients, cover and simmer for 1 hour.

Cook the pasta in plenty of boiling salted water for 15-20 minutes, until tender but not soft. Drain, return to the pan and toss in the butter. Serve the sauce poured over the pasta.

Note Bolognese Sauce is an important part of several more complicated pasta dishes. For example, layer the sauce with cooked lasagne and Cheese Sauce (see page 71) in an ovenproof dish to make a mouth-watering supper. Bake the lasagne in a moderately hot oven (200 C, 400 F, gas 6) for 30-40 minutes, then serve with a green salad.

CABBAGE PARCEL
SERVES 4

4-6 large cabbage leaves
450 g/1 lb chuck steak
150 ml/¼ pint tomato juice
1 teaspoon Worcestershire sauce
few drops of Tabasco sauce
3 tablespoons tomato purée
100 g/4 oz mushrooms
100 g/4 oz breadcrumbs
1 egg
salt and freshly ground black pepper
slices of tomato to garnish
To serve:
Spicy tomato sauce (see page 72)

Blanch the cabbage leaves in boiling, salted water for 1 minute. Drain well and use to line the base and sides of a 1-kg/2-lb loaf tin, reserving one leaf for the top.

Mince the meat, using the double-bladed chopping knife. Add the remaining ingredients and mix again until well combined. Turn the meat mixture into the lined tin, folding the cabbage leaves over to enclose the filling.

Place in a baking tin half filled with water. Cover with foil and bake in a moderate oven (180C, 350F, gas 4) for 1-1¼ hours. Drain off any liquid, turn out and garnish with slices of tomato. Serve hot with tomato sauce.

Variation
Stuffed Cabbage Leaves with Hollandaise Sauce If you like, stuff individual cabbage leaves with the meat mixture. Put them in an ovenproof dish with a little water and bake as above. Serve, garnished with halved lemon slices, with Hollandaise sauce (see page 71).

VEAL FRICADELLES IN CREAM SAUCE
SERVES 4 - 6

450 g/1 lb veal
50 g/2 oz ham
few sprigs parsley
1 egg
salt and freshly ground black pepper
plain flour for coating
25 g/1 oz butter
1 tablespoon oil
5-6 sprigs fresh basil or tarragon
150 ml/¼ pint white wine
150 ml/¼ pint double cream
25 g/1 oz butter

Trim the veal, removing any fat. Finely chop the veal, ham and parsley together, using the double-bladed chopping knife. Add the egg and seasoning and mix well. Shape into rounds about 1 cm/½ in thick. Dredge the rounds with flour, shaking off any excess. Heat the butter and oil and seal the veal patties on both sides. Fry for 15 minutes, turning once during cooking.

Finely chop the basil using the double-bladed chopping knife. Add half the chopped basil to the wine in a pan and bring to the boil. Reduce to about 4 tablespoons then pour in the cream and heat until slightly thickened. Remove from the heat, beat in the butter and remaining basil and pour over the veal

Note Fricadelles can be prepared from leftover cooked meat – veal or pork as well as ham. If you are using leftovers, then finely chop the meat using the double-bladed chopping knife and prepare breadcrumbs from 1 slice of bread in the same way. The breadcrumbs will help to bind the cooked meat together. Continue as in the main recipe.

Stuffed Cabbage Leaves with Hollandaise Sauce

OLIVE PORK PIE
S E R V E S   6

350 g/12oz plain flour
salt and freshly ground black pepper
175 g/6 oz margarine
3 tablespoons water
1 large onion
2 tablespoons oil
225 g/8 oz lean pork
50 g/2 oz streaky bacon, rinds removed
350 g/12 oz sausagemeat
100 g/4 oz stuffed olives
beaten egg to glaze

Mix the flour, a pinch of salt and margarine together, using the double-bladed chopping knife, until the mixture resembles fine breadcrumbs. Add the water and mix to form a dough. Remove from the bowl and knead lightly on a floured surface. Divide the dough in half and leave one half in a cool place. Roll out the other half on a floured surface and use it to line a 19-cm/7½-in square baking tin or an ovenproof dish. Set aside in a cool place.

Peel and quarter the onion and chop finely, using the double-bladed chopping knife. Heat the oil in a pan and fry the onion until tender but not brown. Cut the pork into 2·5-cm/1-in cubes and mince, using the double-bladed chopping knife, until finely ground. Add to the onion. Finely chop the bacon in the same way and add to the pork mixture. Mix the sausagemeat to a smooth paste, using the double-bladed chopping knife. Mix this into the rest of the meat and season to taste. Fry this mixture in its own fat until it is almost cooked and will break into pieces. Remove from the heat and cool slightly. Roughly slice the olives, using the slicing disc, and stir into the meat mixture. Use this to fill the pastry-lined tin. Roll out the rest of the pastry as a lid for the pie; brush the edges of the pastry with water and seal the lid on. Make a small hole in the top of the pie to let steam escape, then brush all over with beaten egg. Bake in a moderately hot oven (200 C, 400 F, gas 6) for 35-40 minutes. Serve hot or cold.

PÂTÉ PIE
S E R V E S   8 - 1 0

275 g/10 oz Hot Water Crust Pastry
(see page 62)
225 g/8 oz raw chicken meat
225 g/8 oz pig's liver
1 medium onion
few sprigs of parsley
1 egg
5 tablespoons fresh breadcrumbs
1 tablespoon tomato purée
salt and freshly ground black pepper
50 g/2 oz shelled hazelnuts
225 g/8 oz pork sausagemeat
½ teaspoon dried sage
1 egg white

Roll out three-quarters of the pastry into a round to line the base and sides of an 18-cm/7-in cake tin. Roll the remaining pastry into a round to use as a lid, reserving a little for decoration.

Cut the chicken into 2.5-cm/1-in pieces and mince, using the double-bladed chopping knife.

Remove from the bowl and set aside. Remove the skin from the liver, peel and quarter the onion and mince together with the parsley and whole egg, using the double-bladed chopping knife. Turn this mixture into a mixing bowl and stir in the breadcrumbs, tomato purée and seasoning.

Use one-third of the liver mixture to make a layer in the base of the pastry-lined tin. Mix the whole hazelnuts with the chicken and use this to make a second layer in the pastry case. Make another layer with half of the remaining liver mixture. Mix the sausagemeat and sage together and season well. Form a fourth layer with the sausagemeat and finish with the remaining liver mixture. Brush the edges of the pastry with water and cover with the pastry lid, pressing the edges together to seal. Make a hole in the centre of the pie for steam to escape, use the remaining pastry pieces for decoration and brush all over with lightly beaten egg white. Cook in a moderately hot oven (200 C, 400 F, gas 6) for 30 minutes then reduce the oven temperature to moderate (180 C, 350 F, gas 4) for a further 1-1½ hours.

Allow the pie to cool in the tin. Turn out and serve cold with salad and French bread.

Olive Pork Pie

PORK BOULANGÈRE
SERVES 4

1 (1·5-kg/3¼-lb) loin of pork, rolled
few sprigs fresh rosemary
675 g/1½ lb potatoes
1 clove garlic, crushed
salt and freshly ground black pepper
75 g/3 oz butter
Garnish:
chopped parsley
watercress

Make small slits in the skin of the pork using a sharp knife and insert a few sprigs of fresh rosemary.

Peel and cut the potatoes in half and slice, using the slicing disc. Arrange some of the potatoes in the base of a casserole dish and spread over the crushed garlic. Sprinkle with a few more sprigs of rosemary and place the pork on top. Add the remaining potatoes around the sides of the meat. Season and dot with butter. Cover and cook in a moderate oven (180 C, 350 F, gas 4) for 1¼ hours. Uncover and increase the oven temperature to moderately hot (200 C, 400 F, gas 6) for a further 30-40 minutes to crisp the outside. Sprinkle the potatoes with the parsley and garnish with a bunch of watercress.

FRENCH LAMB ROAST
SERVES 4

2 courgettes
2 onions
1 green pepper
225 g/8 oz mushrooms
4 tomatoes, peeled
1-2 cloves garlic, crushed
3 tablespoons chopped parsley
salt and freshly ground black pepper
1 (1·5-kg/3¼-lb) leg of lamb

Wash and trim the courgettes and slice, using the slicing disc. Peel and quarter the onions, wash the pepper and remove the seeds. Roughly chop the onions, peppers, mushrooms and tomatoes together, using the double-bladed chopping knife. Combine this mixture with the courgettes, garlic, parsley and seasoning and use this mixture to cover the base of the roasting tin. Place the lamb on top, cover and bake in a moderately hot oven (200 C, 400 F, gas 6) for 1¼-1½ hours. Serve with the cooked vegetables.

French Lamb Roast

Vegetable Dishes

The food processor can be used to transform a few simple vegetables into an exciting accompaniment, tempting supper dish or inexpensive first course. Never again will you be excused from serving plain boiled potatoes or cabbage. The speed with which vegetables can be diced, sliced, chipped or chopped means that they become an interesting feature of the menu whether they are conjured into a warming winter dish or served in the simplest of summer sautées.

POTATOES DAUPHINOISE

SERVES 4

450 g/1 lb potatoes
175 g/6 oz Gruyère cheese
salt and freshly ground black pepper
freshly grated nutmeg
300 ml/½ pint single cream
3 tablespoons chopped parsley to garnish

Peel the potatoes and slice, using the slicing disc. Grate the cheese, using the grating disc. Place alternate layers of potatoes and cheese in an ovenproof dish, adding seasoning and nutmeg between each layer. Pour over the cream and bake in a moderate oven (180C, 350F, gas 4) for 50-60 minutes. Sprinkle with chopped parsley and serve.

GAME CHIPS

SERVES 4

225 g/8 oz potatoes
oil for deep frying

Peel the potatoes and slice thinly, using the slicing disc. Rinse and dry well on kitchen paper. Heat the oil to 185C/360F and fry the chips a few at a time until crisp and golden. Drain well on kitchen paper and serve hot with poultry and game dishes.

ROSTI

SERVES 4

450 g/1 lb potatoes
4 rashers bacon
25 g/1 oz butter
salt and freshly ground black pepper
100 g/4 oz cheese
2 tablespoons chopped parsley to garnish

Peel the potatoes and parboil for 5 minutes. Chop the bacon, using the double-bladed chopping knife and sauté in butter until soft but not crisp.

Grate the potatoes, using the grating disc, season well then add to the bacon. Fry until crisp on both sides.

Grate the cheese, using the grating disc and sprinkle it over the potatoes. Place under a hot grill to melt the cheese and serve sprinkled with the chopped parsley.

Clockwise from top left: Game Chips, Rosti and Potatoes Dauphinoise

SIMPLE VEGETABLE PIE

SERVES 4 - 6

1 quantity Shortcrust pastry (see page 63)
2 large potatoes
4 carrots
2 large onions
225 g/8 oz button mushrooms
salt and freshly ground black pepper
2 tablespoons chopped parsley
1 quantity Onion sauce (see page 71)
beaten egg or milk to glaze

Make the pastry according to the recipe instructions. Roll out to approximately 3·5 cm/1½ in larger than a 1·75-litre/3-pint pie dish. Trim a strip of pastry from the edge to line the rim of the pie dish.

Peel and parboil the potatoes, carrots and onions for 10 minutes then slice thinly using the slicing disc. Layer the vegetables and mushrooms in the dish, seasoning generously between each layer. Stir the parsley into the sauce and carefully pour it over the vegetables encouraging it to run down between the layers.

Dampen the rim of the dish with water and cover with the pastry strip. Dampen the pastry strip with water and top with the pastry lid. Seal the edges and use any trimmings to decorate the pie. Brush with a little beaten egg or milk and bake in a moderate oven (180 C, 350 F, gas 4) for 1 hour. The pie should be golden brown and the vegetables cooked through.

Simple Vegetable Pie and Herby Potato Puffs

HERBY POTATO PUFFS

MAKES 25

1 quantity Choux pastry (see page 62)
50 g/2 oz Cheddar cheese
350 g/12 oz potatoes, boiled and mashed
2 tablespoons chopped fresh herbs
salt and freshly ground black pepper
oil for deep frying

Make the pastry according to the recipe instructions. Grate the cheese coarsely. Beat the potatoes, cheese and herbs into the pastry. Season to taste. Heat the oil in a deep frying pan and deep fry spoonfuls of the mixture until crisp and golden brown, about 3-5 minutes.

BEANS PROVENÇAL

SERVES 4

1 small onion
50 g/2 oz streaky bacon
50 g/2 oz mushrooms
15 g/½ oz butter
1 clove garlic, crushed
15 g/½ oz plain flour
1 (396-g/14-oz) can tomatoes
few drops of Worcestershire sauce
few drops of Tabasco sauce
salt and freshly ground black pepper
450 g/1 lb French beans
grated Parmesan cheese

Peel and quarter the onion, then chop finely using the double-bladed chopping knife. Remove from the bowl and set aside. Roughly chop the bacon and mushrooms, using the doubled-bladed chopping knife.

Melt the butter in a saucepan and lightly sauté the onion, bacon, mushrooms and crushed garlic until soft. Sprinkle with the flour, stir well and cook for a few minutes.

Strain the can of tomatoes and purée the fruit until smooth, using the double-bladed chopping knife. Add the purée to the mixture in the saucepan with the sauces and seasoning. Cook, stirring, for 5 minutes.

Meanwhile, trim the French beans and cook in boiling salted water until tender about 10 minutes. Toss the beans in the hot tomato sauce, sprinkle with the grated Parmesan cheese and serve immediately.

VEGETABLE CURRY

S E R V E S 4

1 large onion
100 g/4 oz carrots
1 large parsnip (optional)
3 tablespoons oil
2 cloves garlic, crushed
2 tablespoons garam masala
½ teaspoon turmeric
100 g/4 oz mushrooms
1 small cauliflower
100 g/4 oz French beans
100 g/4 oz frozen peas
1 (425-g/15-oz) can chopped tomatoes
150 ml/¼ pint chicken stock
salt and freshly ground black pepper
To serve:
½ cucumber
150 ml/¼ pint natural yogurt

Peel and quarter the onion, then peel the carrots and parsnip (if used). Slice these ingredients using the slicing disc. Heat the oil in a large flameproof casserole, add the sliced vegetables and garlic and cook until soft but not browned.

Meanwhile, clean and roughly chop the mushrooms using the double-bladed knife. Add the garam masala and turmeric to the fried vegetables and cook for a few minutes. Break the cauliflower into florets, trim the French beans and add both to the pan with the peas, tomatoes and stock. Stir well, adding seasoning to taste, and bring to the boil. Cover and simmer very gently for 30-40 minutes.

Peel and chop the cucumber using the double-bladed chopping knife, then mix it with the yogurt. Transfer the vegetable curry to a warmed serving platter and top with the cucumber and yogurt mixture. Serve at once, with plain boiled rice.

RED CABBAGE CASSEROLE

S E R V E S 6

1 kg/2¼ lb red cabbage
2 onions
2 cooking apples
2 tablespoons soft brown sugar
2 tablespoons orange juice
3 tablespoons red wine vinegar
150 ml/¼ pint chicken stock
salt and freshly ground black pepper

Remove the coarse outer leaves of the cabbage, together with the thick stalk. Cut the cabbage into wedges which will fit into the feed tube and slice, using the slicing disc. Peel the onions and slice in the same way. Peel, core and chop the apples, using the double-bladed chopping knife.

Place layers of cabbage, onion and apple in an oven-proof casserole dish. Add the remaining ingredients, cover and bake in a moderately hot oven (200 C, 400 F, gas 6) for 50-60 minutes.

Vegetable Curry

VEGETABLE LASAGNE
SERVES 6 - 8

225 g/8 oz aubergines
1 medium onion
2 sticks celery
2 medium courgettes
600 ml/1 pint stock
50 g/2 oz plain flour
50 g/2 oz butter
300 ml/½ pint milk
¼ teaspoon celery salt
freshly ground black pepper
225 g/8 oz lasagne
175 g/6 oz Cheddar cheese

Peel and halve the aubergines, sprinkle them with salt and leave to stand for 30 minutes.

Peel the onion, clean the celery and trim the courgettes. Rinse and dry the aubergines and slice, with the other prepared vegetables, using the slicing disc. Simmer the vegetables in the stock for 10-15 minutes, then strain and reserve 300 ml/½ pint of the stock. Cool the stock and pour together with the flour, butter, milk, celery salt and black pepper into the bowl and mix well until smooth, using the double-bladed chopping knife. Pour this sauce mixture into a pan, bring to the boil slowly, stirring all the time, then simmer for 2 minutes.

Meanwhile cook the lasagne in boiling salted water, according to the directions on the packet.

Place a layer of cooked lasagne in the base of a 1·5-litre/2½-pint ovenproof dish. Cover this with half the cooked vegetables and then a layer of sauce. Grate the cheese, using the grating disc and sprinkle half of it over the sauce. Repeat these layers, ending with a layer of sauce covered with the remaining grated cheese. Bake in a moderate oven (180 C, 350 F, gas 4) for 30 minutes. If necessary brown the cheese under the grill before serving.

COURGETTES AU GRATIN
SERVES 4

1 small onion
1 clove garlic
50 g/2 oz butter
1 slice white bread, crusts removed
675 g/1½ lb courgettes
1 teaspoon lemon juice
salt and freshly ground black pepper
100 g/4 oz Cheddar cheese
chopped parsley to garnish

Peel the onion and garlic and chop roughly, using the double-bladed chopping knife. Melt the butter and fry the onion and garlic until soft, but not browned. Make breadcrumbs, using the double-bladed chopping knife.

Trim the courgettes, place in the feed tube and slice, using the slicing disc. Sauté them in the butter with the onion for about 5 minutes. Add the lemon juice and seasoning and place in an ovenproof dish.

Grate the cheese, using the grating disc, and mix together with the breadcrumbs. Sprinkle this over the courgettes and bake in a moderate oven (180 C, 350 F, gas 4) for 30-35 minutes. Garnish with chopped parsley and serve hot.

Variation
You can, if you like, add chopped fresh basil or marjoram to the courgettes when you transfer them to the ovenproof dish. If fresh herbs are not available substitute dried oregano or marjoram.

PROVENÇAL ONIONS
SERVES 4

4 medium onions
4 slices white bread, crusts removed
1 clove garlic, crushed
salt and freshly ground black pepper
50 g/2 oz cheese, grated
1 egg, beaten
25 g/1 oz butter
chopped parsley to garnish
Spicy tomato sauce (see page 72)

Peel and cook the onions in boiling salted water for 15-20 minutes, without overcooking. Drain and cool.

Make breadcrumbs, using the double-bladed chopping knife. Add the garlic, seasoning and half the cheese and mix well.

Scoop out the centres of the onions, chop finely and mix with the breadcrumb mixture. Moisten with the beaten egg. Stuff the onions and place in a greased ovenproof dish. Top with butter and the remaining cheese. Cook in a moderate oven (180 C, 350 F, gas 4) for 20-30 minutes. Garnish and serve with Spicy tomato sauce.

PEPPER AND ONION PICKLE
MAKES 1.5 - 1.75 kg / 3 - 4 lb

4 large green peppers
1 kg/2 lb onions
225 g/8 oz cooking dates
350 g/12 oz granulated sugar
300 ml/½ pint tarragon vinegar
1 teaspoon salt

Quarter the peppers, remove the seeds and chop roughly, using the double-bladed chopping knife. Peel and quarter the onions, chop roughly in the same way and place in a large saucepan with the chopped pepper. Cut the dates into small pieces and chop, using the double-bladed chopping knife. Add to the peppers and onions together with all the other ingredients. Stir well.

Bring the mixture to the boil then reduce the heat, cover and simmer for 1½-1¾ hours. Pour the pickle into warmed sterilised jars and cover while hot.

MARROW CHUTNEY
MAKES 2.25 kg / 5 lb

1 (1.75-kg/4-lb) marrow, seeds removed
and peeled
175 g/6 oz salt
450 g/1 lb onions
450 g/1 lb cooking apples
350 g/12 oz soft brown sugar
350 g/12 oz sultanas
600 ml/1 pint vinegar

Cut the marrow into large chunks and chop roughly using the double-bladed chopping knife. Place layers of the chopped marrow in a large bowl and sprinkle each layer generously with the salt. Cover and leave to stand overnight. Drain the liquid from the marrow, and rinse off the remaining salt. Drain and place in a large saucepan.

Peel and quarter the onions and chop roughly, using the double-bladed chopping knife. Add to the saucepan with the marrow. Peel and core the cooking apples and chop roughly, using the double-bladed chopping knife. Add to the marrow and onion together with the remaining ingredients.

Bring the mixture to the boil then simmer for 45 minutes or until the chutney is soft and thick. Turn into dry, sterilised jars which have been warmed. Cover the chutney while it is still hot.

Provençal Onions

SPINACH AND NUTMEG CROQUETTES

SERVES 4

100 g/4 oz butter
100 g/4 oz plain flour
300 ml/½ pint milk
salt and freshly ground black pepper
50 g/2 oz Cheddar cheese
¼ teaspoon freshly grated nutmeg
450 g/1 lb spinach
1 egg, lightly beaten
4 tablespoons milk
75 g/3 oz dried white breadcrumbs
oil for deep frying

Melt the butter in a large saucepan and stir in the flour. Cook for a few minutes, then gradually stir in the milk and continue cooking until very thick. Season and cook for a further 2 minutes. Grate the cheese, using the grating disc, and stir into the cooked mixture with the nutmeg. Leave to cool. Trim the spinach and cook in boiling salted water until just tender. Drain well and chop finely, using the double-bladed chopping knife. Beat the spinach into the cheese sauce, adjust the seasoning, then spread the mixture over the base of a greased Swiss roll tin to a depth of about 1 cm/½ in. Chill until set firmly.

Mark the mixture into nine squares, then shape each piece into a croquette shape on a lightly floured board. Mix the egg and milk together and dip each croquette in the mixture. Coat each one in breadcrumbs and leave in the refrigerator for at least 30 minutes to allow the coating to harden.

Heat the fat to 185 C/360 F and fry the croquettes until the coating is crisp and golden. Serve immediately with Spicy tomato sauce (see page 72).

Variation
Carrot and Cheese Croquettes Substitute 225 g/8 oz carrots for the spinach in the above recipe. Parboil and finely grate the cooled carrots, then beat them into the sauce and continue as above.

CARROTS IN CREAM AND WINE SAUCE

SERVES 4

450 g/1 lb carrots
2 bunches spring onions
50 g/2 oz butter
1 tablespoon soft brown sugar
salt and freshly ground black pepper
pinch of cayenne
1 teaspoon dried oregano
150 ml/¼ pint white wine
150 ml/5 fl oz soured cream
2 tablespoons chopped parsley to garnish

Peel the carrots and slice, using the slicing disc. Trim the onions down to the bulb. Melt the butter and sauté the carrots and onions for 5 minutes. Stir in the sugar, seasoning, cayenne, oregano and white wine. Cover and simmer for 20-25 minutes. Just before serving, spoon the soured cream on top and sprinkle with the chopped parsley.

Note Parsnips can be cooked in the above recipe. Peel and slice the parsnips in the same way as the carrots and cook as in the recipe. Add a little freshly grated nutmeg to the vegetables just before serving.

Spinach and Nutmeg Croquettes and Carrots in Cream and Wine Sauce

Salads

The secret of a good salad lies in the speedy preparation of fresh ingredients. These should be evenly chopped or sliced so that the flavours mingle well. Chopped herbs and a thoroughly mixed, full-flavoured dressing will complete the salad.
Whether you are preparing a side salad or a main course dish, you will find that the preparation time is reduced considerably once you bring your food processor into play.

COURGETTE SALAD

SERVES 4

100 g/4 oz button mushrooms
450 g/1 lb courgettes
225 g/8 oz garlic sausage, in 1 piece
small bunch parsley
grated rind and juice of 1 lemon
5 tablespoons salad oil
½ teaspoon salt
1 teaspoon sugar
½ teaspoon mustard powder
freshly ground black pepper
3 tomatoes, peeled

Clean the mushrooms and thinly peel the courgettes. Slice both thickly using the slicing disc. Cut the garlic sausage into even strips. Mix the mushrooms, courgettes and garlic sausage together. Chop the parsley, using the double-bladed chopping knife. Add the lemon rind and juice, the oil, salt, sugar and mustard. Season well with pepper. Mix well until the ingredients are emulsified. Pour this dressing over the courgette mixture and toss well. Cover and leave to stand for about 1 hour. Cut the tomatoes into wedges and toss into the salad before serving.

SPINACH SALAD

SERVES 4

450 g/1 lb fresh spinach
1 bunch spring onions
salt and freshly ground black pepper
freshly grated nutmeg
4 tablespoons oil
1 tablespoon white wine vinegar or lemon juice
2 hard-boiled eggs to garnish

Remove and discard any coarse stems from the spinach, then chop roughly, using the double-bladed chopping knife. Trim the spring onions and chop. Mix with the spinach and add seasoning and nutmeg to taste. Mix the oil and vinegar together thoroughly. Pour over the spinach and toss gently. Taste and adjust the seasoning.

Chop the eggs, using the double-bladed chopping knife, and sprinkle over the spinach.

SAGE DERBY COLESLAW

SERVES 6 - 8

75 g/3 oz Sage Derby cheese
50 g/2 oz blanched almonds
50 g/2 oz cucumber
350 g/12 oz white cabbage
1 green pepper
2 dessert apples
little lemon juice
150 ml/¼ pint Basic mayonnaise (see page 70)
salt and freshly ground black pepper
2 tablespoons chopped parsley

Roughly chop the cheese, using the double-bladed chopping knife. Transfer the cheese to a large mixing bowl. Chop the blanched almonds finely, using the double-bladed chopping knife, and add to the cheese. Peel the cucumber, chop roughly in the same way and add to the mixing bowl.

Cut the cabbage into wedges which will pass through the feed tube, and slice finely, using the slicing disc. Cut the green pepper into quarters lengthways, remove the seeds and slice finely, using the slicing disc.

Add the cabbage and pepper to the cheese, almonds and cucumber in the mixing bowl.

Peel, core and quarter the apples. Slice, using the slicing disc and sprinkle liberally with lemon juice to prevent discoloration. Add to the cabbage mixture.

Stir the mayonnaise, seasoning and chopped parsley into the coleslaw and mix well.

Variation

There are several ways in which the basic coleslaw recipe can be varied. Adding a well-flavoured cheese, as above, turns the salad into an interesting supper dish. For a spicy side salad, shred cabbage, onion and green pepper with celery and carrots. Dress the salad with oil, vinegar, chilli powder and Tabasco sauce, adding a generous pinch of dried mixed herbs. (Illustrated on title page)

CRUNCHY WALDORF SALAD

SERVES 4

½ cucumber
few sprigs parsley
75 g/3 oz walnuts
3 sticks celery
4 dessert apples
little lemon juice
150 ml/¼ pint Basic mayonnaise (see page 70)
few crisp lettuce leaves (optional)
Garnish:
¼ dessert apple, thinly sliced
few walnut halves
celery leaves or lettuce leaves

Peel the cucumber and chop roughly, using the double-bladed chopping knife, together with the parsley, walnuts and celery. Core the apples and chop roughly in the same way, adding a little lemon juice to prevent discoloration. Mix all the ingredients together with the mayonnaise. Line a dish with the lettuce, pile the salad on top, garnish and serve.

AVOCADO AND ORANGE SALAD

SERVES 4

few sprigs of parsley
grated rind of 1 orange
3 tablespoons orange juice
1 tablespoon white wine vinegar
6 tablespoons oil
salt and freshly ground black pepper
2 ripe avocados
2 small dessert pears

Chop the parsley, using the double-bladed chopping knife. Add the orange rind, juice, vinegar, oil and seasoning to the bowl and mix well. Pour the dressing into a basin. Cut the avocados lengthways, remove the stones and carefully scoop out the flesh, leaving the skins undamaged. Cut into small cubes, and add to the dressing. Peel, core and quarter the pears. Chop into cubes and stir in the avocado and dressing. Divide this filling between the avocado shells and serve immediately.

Crunchy Waldorf Salad and Avocado and Orange Salad

MUSHROOMS À LA GRECQUE
S E R V E S 4

1 onion
25 g/1 oz butter
1 clove garlic, crushed
150 ml/¼ pint white wine
225 g/8 oz mushrooms
4 tomatoes, peeled
salt and freshly ground black pepper
chopped parsley to garnish

Peel and quarter the onion and chop finely, using the double-bladed chopping knife. Sauté in the butter until soft, add the crushed garlic and wine and bring to the boil.

Slice the mushrooms, using the slicing disc, then add to the wine. Simmer gently for 2-3 minutes. Cut the tomatoes into quarters and stir in with the mushrooms. Season to taste then chill thoroughly before serving. Garnish with chopped parsley.

CUCUMBER SALAD
S E R V E S 4

1 cucumber
salt, to sprinkle
French Dressing (see Pasta Salad, right)
3 tablespoons chopped parsley
2 sprigs fresh dill
soured cream

Peel the cucumber and slice thinly, using the slicing disc. Sprinkle the cucumber with salt and leave for 30-60 minutes. Rinse well and drain. Toss in the French dressing and chill. Just before serving, sprinkle with the chopped parsley and sprigs of dill and serve with soured cream.

PASTA SALAD
S E R V E S 4 - 6

225 g/8 oz pasta shapes
1 small onion
50 g/2 oz streaky bacon
15 g/½ oz butter
50 g/2 oz mushrooms
2 hard-boiled eggs
2 tablespoons chopped parsley
1 tablespoon chopped chives
Dressing:
4 tablespoons oil
1 tablespoon white wine vinegar or lemon juice
pinch of mustard powder
salt and freshly ground black pepper

Cook the pasta in boiling salted water until tender. Meanwhile mix the dressing ingredients together thoroughly. Drain the pasta well and toss in the dressing. Set aside to cool.

Peel and quarter the onion and chop finely with the bacon, using the double-bladed chopping knife.

Melt the butter in a pan and gently sauté the onion and bacon. Roughly chop the mushrooms, using the double-bladed chopping knife, and add to the onion and bacon. Continue to fry this mixture gently until soft. Strain off any excess fat, then add the mixture to the pasta.

Roughly chop the hard-boiled eggs, using the double-bladed chopping knife. Stir into the pasta mixture together with the chopped herbs. Adjust the seasoning and serve cold.

Desserts

Sorbets, ice creams, flans, soufflés and cheesecakes can all be made quite effortlessly with the aid of a food processor, as it is such an excellent way to purée fruit really smoothly. Delightful and interesting flavours can be combined to provide a delicious end to any meal. Use the machine for all the pastry bases and for decoration too – nuts, chocolate or crystallised fruit can be quickly chopped or grated to add that special, last-minute touch.

APPLE AND ALMOND PUFF

SERVES 6 - 8

1 (212-g/7½-oz) packet puff pastry
100 g/4 oz dried apricots, soaked overnight
450 g/1 lb cooking apples
40 g/1½ oz brown sugar
¼ teaspoon ground cloves
grated rind of ½ lemon
lightly beaten egg for brushing
castor sugar to sprinkle
Almond paste:
100 g/4 oz ground almonds
50 g/2 oz castor sugar
50 g/2 oz icing sugar
½ teaspoon lemon juice
½ egg, lightly beaten

Roll the pastry to an oblong 25×30 cm/10×12 in and place on a dampened baking tray.

To make the almond paste, mix all the ingredients together, using the double-bladed chopping knife. Turn out onto a board lightly dusted with icing sugar, and knead lightly. Roll out to an oblong 2.5 cm/1 in smaller than the pastry and lay it on top. Set aside and chill.

Chop the apricots roughly, using the double-bladed chopping knife. Peel, core and slice the apples, using the slicing disc, by placing a few quarters at a time in the feed tube, then pressing down lightly with the plastic pusher. Mix the apricots, apples, brown sugar, ground cloves and grated lemon rind in a mixing bowl and arrange this filling down the centre of the pastry. Bring the long sides of the pastry to the centre of the filling. Overlap the edges of the pastry and seal them together with water.

Turn the roll over so that the seam is underneath. Close the ends of the pastry roll and fold them underneath. Decorate with any remaining pastry trimmings. Brush with beaten egg and sprinkle with castor sugar. Bake in a moderately hot oven (200C, 400F, gas 6) for 35 minutes. Serve hot or cold with clotted cream.

APPLE AND PEACH AMBER

SERVES 4 - 6

4 fresh peaches
450 g/1 lb cooking apples
juice of ½ lemon
100 g/4 oz demerara sugar
Topping:
50 g/2 oz butter or margarine
50 g/2 oz castor sugar
1 egg
50 g/2 oz self-raising flour
½ teaspoon baking powder

Peel and halve or quarter the peaches, remove their stones then slice them using the slicing disc. Peel and core the apples, cut them into quarters then slice them using the slicing disc. Mix the fruit in an ovenproof dish, sprinkle with lemon juice and stir in the sugar.

Use the double-bladed knife to make the topping: place all the ingredients in the bowl and process until creamy. Spread the mixture over the fruit and bake in a moderate oven (180C, 350F, gas 4) for 50-60 minutes, until risen and golden brown.

Apple and Peach Amber

TROPICAL FRUIT FLAN

SERVES 6

350 g/12 oz Shortcrust pastry (see page 63)
1 small pineapple
50 g/2 oz fresh or desiccated coconut
1 dessert apple
50 g/2 oz sugar
2 teaspoons cornflour
beaten egg to glaze

Roll out three-quarters of the pastry and use to line a 23-cm/9-in flan ring. Bake blind in a moderately hot oven (200 C, 400 F, gas 6) for 10 minutes.

Meanwhile, trim and peel the pineapple. Remove the eyes and core, then cut the fruit into chunks and chop it finely using the double-bladed chopping knife. If using fresh coconut, grate it finely using the grating disc. Peel, core and quarter the apple then grate it finely in the same way.

Mix the fruit with the coconut and sugar. Blend the cornflour with a little of the juices from the fruit, then stir it into the mixture. Turn the fruit filling into the flan. Roll out the remaining pastry thinly into an oblong shape, then cut it into 1-cm/½-in wide strips. Twist the strips of pastry and arrange them in a lattice pattern over the filling. Secure the ends of the strips to the edge of the flan with a little beaten egg and trim off any excess pastry. Brush with a little beaten egg and bake for a further 20-30 minutes. Serve hot or cold, with cream or ice cream.

CHEESE APPLE FLAN
S E R V E S   6 - 8

225 g/8 oz Shortcrust pastry (see page 63)
2 tablespoons apricot jam
450 g/1 lb cooking apples
50 g/2 oz soft brown sugar
75 g/3 oz Cheshire cheese
egg white for brushing

Roll out three-quarters of the pastry and use it to line a 23-cm/9-in flan ring. Bake blind in a moderately hot oven (200 C, 400 F, gas 6) for 15 minutes. Spread the apricot jam over the base of the flan.

Peel, core and slice the apples, using the slicing disc as described in the recipe for Apple and almond puff (page 52). Arrange the slices in the flan ring and sprinkle with the sugar.

Crumble the cheese into the bowl and chop finely, using the double-bladed chopping knife. Sprinkle over the flan.

Roll out the remaining pastry and cut into strips. Arrange the strips in a lattice pattern over the flan. Brush over with lightly beaten egg white. Bake in a moderately hot oven (200 C, 400 F, gas 6) for a further 20-30 minutes. Serve hot with cream.

Variations
Wholemeal Cheese and Apple Flan Substitute wholemeal pastry in the above recipe.
Raisin, Cheese and Apple Flan Sprinkle 50 g/2 oz raisins over the apples before adding the sugar.
Nutty Cheese and Apple Flan Sprinkle 100 g/4 oz chopped walnuts over the apples before adding the sugar.

STRAWBERRY CHEESECAKE
S E R V E S   6 - 8

225 g/8 oz Sweet wholemeal pastry
(see page 63)
225 g/8 oz fresh strawberries
225 g/8 oz cottage cheese
150 ml/5 fl oz soured cream
2 eggs, separated
75 g/3 oz castor sugar
15 g/½ oz gelatine
3 tablespoons warm water
grated rind and juice of 1 lemon
Decoration:
whipped cream
few strawberries, halved

Roll out the pastry and use to line a 23-cm/9-inch fluted flan ring. Prick the base and bake blind in a moderately hot oven (200 C, 400 F, gas 6) for 15-20 minutes. Remove the paper lining and reduce the oven temperature to moderate (180 C, 350 F, gas 4) for a further 10-15 minutes. Leave to cool.

Hull and purée the strawberries, using the double-bladed chopping knife. Add the cottage cheese, soured cream, egg yolks and sugar, and beat together.

Soften the gelatine in the warm water. Stir well in a bowl over hot water until the gelatine has completely dissolved. Cool slightly, then pour into the strawberry mixture through the feed tube, mixing all the time with the double-bladed chopping knife.

Beat the egg whites until stiff, then fold carefully into the fruit and cheese mixture. Pour into the cooked flan case and chill until set. Decorate with whipped cream and halved strawberries.

LIME SPLICE

SERVES 6 - 8

1 (200-g/7-oz) packet ginger nuts
50 g/2 oz butter, melted
grated rind and juice of 1 lime
lime cordial
2 teaspoons cornflour
50 g/2 oz castor sugar
1 egg, separated
150 ml/¼ pint double cream
Decoration:
slices of lime
whipped cream

Roughly break up the ginger nuts and make into fine crumbs, using the double-bladed chopping knife. Pour the melted butter through the feed tube and mix for a few seconds. Use the mixture to line the base and sides of a 20-cm/8-in flan dish. Press the crumbs down firmly and leave to chill.

Make up the juice of the lime to 75 ml/3 fl oz with lime cordial. Then make the mixture up to 150 ml/¼ pint with water.

Pour a little onto the cornflour and mix well. Heat the remaining juice. When hot pour onto the cornflour mixture, mix well and return to the heat to thicken. Add the grated lime rind and sugar. Allow to cool slightly then beat in the egg yolk. When the mixture is completely cold, lightly whip the cream and fold it into the mixture. Whisk the egg white and fold it also into the mixture. Pour into the chilled biscuit case and decorate with slices of lime and whipped cream.

COEUR À L'ORANGE

SERVES 8

225 g/8 oz cottage cheese
300 ml/½ pint double cream
4 tablespoons fresh orange juice
50 g/2 oz castor sugar
2 egg whites
Decoration:
slices of orange
mint leaves (optional)

Mash the cottage cheese, using the double-bladed chopping knife, until really smooth. Lightly whip the cream and orange juice together until soft but not stiff. Add to the cheese with the sugar and mix until well combined. Whisk the egg whites until stiff and fold into the cream mixture with a metal spoon. Divide the mixture between eight special heart-shaped moulds with holes in the base for draining. Alternatively use eight individual ramekin dishes and tie a piece of muslin over the top of each, then turn upside down on a plate. Allow to drain overnight before serving. Either serve in the moulds or turn out and decorate with slices of orange and mint leaves.

PEACH ICE CREAM

SERVES 6

450 ml/¾ pint milk
175 g/6 oz castor sugar
2 eggs
300 ml/½ pint double cream
6 peaches

Whisk the milk, sugar and eggs together in a mixing bowl until well combined. Stand the bowl over a saucepan of hot water and cook until slightly thickened, stirring occasionally. Allow to cool.

Stir in the double cream and pour into a shallow freezer container. Partially freeze until slushy.

Skin the peaches, remove the stones and purée, using the double-bladed chopping knife. Add the partially frozen mixture and mix well. Return to the freezer until partially frozen. Using the double-bladed chopping knife, mix the ice cream until smooth and light in colour. Return the ice cream to the freezer and freeze until firm. Remove from the freezer and place in the refrigerator 1 hour before serving.

Variation
Chocolate Hazelnut Ice Cream Prepare the basic ice cream mixture as in the above recipe omitting the peaches. Dissolve 4 tablespoons cocoa powder in 4 tablespoons boiling water, allow to cool slightly, then stir this flavouring into the ice cream mixture. Add 50 g/2 oz chopped toasted hazelnuts and freeze as in the main recipe. Serve the ice cream scooped into dishes and pipe a swirl of whipped cream onto each portion. Add a few lightly toasted, blanched whole hazelnuts to each portion before serving.

From the top: Peach Ice Cream, Coeur à l'Orange and Lime Splice

GOOSEBERRY ICE CREAM

SERVES 6 - 8

450 g/1 lb gooseberries, defrosted if frozen
100 g/4 oz castor sugar
3 eggs, separated
300 ml/½ pint double cream
grated rind of ½ lemon

Cook the gooseberries in their own juices with 50 g/ 2 oz of the sugar until just tender. Purée, using the double-bladed chopping knife and cool. Sieve to remove seeds, if desired.

Put the egg yolks and two of the whites into the bowl. Add the rest of the sugar and 250 ml/8 fl oz of the cream. Mix well, using the double-bladed chopping knife. Transfer to a mixing bowl and place over a pan of gently simmering water. Stir until the custard coats the back of the spoon and cool.

Whip the remaining cream lightly and whisk the egg white until stiff. Mix the fruit and lemon rind into the cooled custard. Fold in the cream and egg white with a metal spoon. Turn into a polythene container and freeze until firm. Allow to soften in the refrigerator for 1-2 hours before serving.

Variation

Pineapple Bombe Omit the gooseberries from the above recipe. Purée 2 (376-g/13¼-oz) cans crushed pineapple with half the amount of sugar. Use this purée instead of the gooseberry purée and make the ice cream as in the main recipe.

Freeze the ice cream in a pudding basin, then dip it briefly in hot water and invert the ice cream onto a serving platter. Decorate with whipped cream and chopped toasted nuts. Soften the bombe in the refrigerator for about 30-60 minutes before serving.

PLUM AND GINGER SORBET

SERVES 4

450 g/1 lb firm yellow plums
100 g/4 oz castor sugar
25 g/1 oz crystallised ginger, chopped
4 egg whites
Decoration:
whipped cream
chopped nuts

Peel and stone the plums then purée them, using the double-bladed chopping knife. Transfer the purée to a bowl and stir in the sugar and ginger. Freeze this mixture until it is just firm.

Whisk the egg whites until stiff. Mash the plum and ginger mixture to break down the ice crystals. Fold in the egg whites and refreeze. Remove the sorbet from the freezer 30 minutes before it is required. Serve in glasses, decorated with whipped cream and chopped nuts.

Pineapple Bombe

TIPSY GALA RING
SERVES 6

150 ml/¼ pint water
50 g/2 oz butter
65 g/2½ oz plain flour, sieved
2 eggs, beaten
25 g/1 oz flaked almonds
castor sugar to sprinkle
Filling:
300 ml/½ pint double cream
3 tablespoons Cointreau
3 fresh peaches
grated rind of ½ orange
Decoration:
icing sugar

Put the water and butter in a saucepan. When the butter has melted, bring the liquid quickly to the boil. Remove from the heat and beat in the flour. Continue to cook for a few seconds until the mixture comes away from the side of the pan. Allow to cool.

Turn the mixture into the bowl, fitted with the double-bladed chopping knife. Gradually add the beaten eggs through the feed tube, mixing all the time. Use the mixture to fill a piping bag, fitted with a plain 2.5-cm/1-in nozzle, and pipe a 23-cm/9-in ring onto a greased baking tray. Sprinkle the top with the almonds and a little sugar. Bake in a moderately hot oven (200 C, 400 F, gas 6) for 20 minutes. Reduce the temperature to moderate (180 C, 350 F, gas 4) for a further 20-25 minutes. Remove from the oven and cool on a wire tray.

For the filling, whip the cream and Cointreau together. Peel and chop the peaches and fold into the cream with the orange rind. Split the choux ring and fill with the cream mixture. Dust the top with icing sugar.

To Peel Peaches Place the fruit in a bowl and pour on freshly boiling water to cover. Leave for 1 minute, then drain and peel the peaches – the skin will come off easily. To prevent peaches from discolouring, sprinkle the cut fruit with a little lemon juice.

SPICED COFFEE SOUFFLÉ
SERVES 4

25 g/1 oz butter
25 g/1 oz plain flour
150 ml/¼ pint milk
50 g/2 oz castor sugar
4 eggs, separated
¼ teaspoon mixed spice
2 tablespoons instant coffee

Place the butter, flour and milk in the bowl and mix until smooth, using the double-bladed chopping knife. Transfer to a saucepan and bring to the boil, stirring continuously. Cook until thick. Stir in the sugar and cook for a further 2 minutes.

Return the sauce to the bowl and add the egg yolks, mixed spice and coffee, dissolved in 2 teaspoons of hot water. Mix until smooth, using the double-bladed chopping knife.

Meanwhile whisk the egg whites until stiff. Add half the egg whites to the sauce in the bowl and mix them in well, using the double-bladed chopping knife. Transfer the mixture to a mixing bowl and fold in the remaining egg whites with a metal spoon.

Pour the soufflé mixture into a greased 1·25-litre/2-pint soufflé dish and bake in a moderately hot oven (190 C, 375 F, gas 5) for 35-40 minutes. Serve at once.

Tipsy Gala Ring

Baking

Whether you are making feather-light cakes and pastries, bread doughs or a simple butter icing, the food processor can beat, knead or cream for you in seconds. Extreme care must be taken not to overmix, so keep stopping the machine at regular intervals to check. Some machines have a plastic blade which is suitable for mixtures requiring minimal mixing. Otherwise use the double-bladed chopping knife. Always remember to check the capacity of the bowl or container before beginning a recipe.

BASIC CHOUX PASTRY

MAKES 150ml / ¼ pint

50 g/2 oz butter
150 ml/¼ pint water
65 g/2½ oz plain flour, sieved
2 eggs

Place the butter and water in a saucepan and heat gently until the butter has melted. Bring quickly to the boil, remove from the heat and beat in the flour. Return to the heat and cook, stirring all the time for 1 minute. Allow to cool.

Beat the eggs lightly. Place the cooled mixture in the bowl and, using the double-bladed chopping knife, gradually pour in the beaten eggs, a little at a time. Mix to a stiffish paste. Use as required.

Variation

Cheese Choux Pastry   Grate 25 g/1 oz cheese, using the grating disc, and add to the mixture before adding the eggs.

HOT WATER CRUST PASTRY

MAKES 275g / 10oz

75 g/3 oz margarine
150 ml/¼ pint water
175 g/10 oz plain flour
½ teaspoon salt
1 egg yolk

Heat the margarine and water together in a saucepan until the margarine has melted, then bring rapidly to the boil. Place the remaining ingredients in the bowl and pour the hot liquid through the feed tube. Mix to a dough, using the double-bladed chopping knife. Turn out onto a floured board and knead lightly until smooth. Leave to rest in a polythene bag for 30 minutes. Use as required.

SHORTCRUST PASTRY

MAKES 225g/8oz

225 g/8 oz plain flour
100 g/4 oz margarine or butter,
cut into cubes
2-3 tablespoons water

Using the double-bladed chopping knife, mix the flour and margarine together until the mixture resembles fine breadcrumbs. Add the water through the feed tube and mix to form a dough. Knead lightly on a floured board and use as required.

Variations

Wholemeal Pastry   Substitute plain wholemeal flour for the white flour.

Sweet Wholemeal Pastry   Add 25 g/1 oz castor sugar to the above recipe.

Cheese Pastry   Grate 50 g/2 oz cheese, using the grating disc, and add to the flour with a pinch of mustard powder and cayenne.

Herb Pastry   Finely chop a handful of mixed fresh herbs (parsley, thyme, marjoram, tarragon, mint or rosemary) using the double-bladed chopping knife.

Add the flour and fat to the herbs and continue as in the main recipe.

Savoury Nut Pastry   Grate 50 g/2 oz mature Cheddar cheese, using the grating disc, and chop 50 g/2 oz salted peanuts. Add to the flour with a pinch of mustard powder.

Sweet Shortcrust   Add 25 g/1 oz castor sugar to the above recipe and use 1 egg yolk instead of the water.

Sweet Almond Pastry   Substitute 50 g/2 oz ground almonds for an equal quantity of the flour. Add 25 g/1 oz castor sugar to the dry ingredients and substitute an egg yolk for the water. Add a few drops of almond essence to the egg.

CHEESE AND ONION ROLLS
MAKES 8 ROLLS

1 small onion
15 g/½ oz butter
50 g/2 oz cheese
1 tablespoon dried yeast
150 ml/¼ pint warm milk
225 g/8 oz plain flour
pinch of salt
1 teaspoon mustard powder
beaten egg to glaze

Peel and quarter the onion, and chop finely, using the double-bladed chopping knife. Sauté the onion in the butter until soft. Grate the cheese, using the grating disc. Sprinkle the dried yeast onto the milk and leave in a warm place until frothy.

Place the flour and seasonings in the bowl with the cooked onion and grated cheese. Pour the yeast mixture through the feed tube and mix, using the double-bladed chopping knife, to form a dough. Cover and leave in a warm place until doubled in size – about 1 hour. Turn onto a floured board and knead lightly.

Divide into eight portions and shape into long rolls. Place side by side in a greased 1-kg/2-lb loaf tin, so that the rolls touch each other. Cover and leave to rise in a warm place for 30 minutes. Brush with beaten egg, then bake in a moderately hot oven (200 C, 400 F, gas 6) for 20-25 minutes.

Variation

To make plain, rich finger rolls, omit the cheese and mustard from the above recipe. Prepare and bake the dough as above. These rolls are an excellent accompaniment to a first course or they can be served with pâté and cheese for a light lunch. (Illustrated on title page)

GRANARY LOAF
MAKES 1 (450-g/1-lb) LOAF

¾ teaspoon dried yeast
150 ml/¼ pint warm water
½ teaspoon castor sugar
100 g/4 oz granary flour
100 g/4 oz plain wholemeal flour
pinch of salt
15 g/½ oz butter
cracked wheat

Sprinkle the yeast onto the warm water and stir in the sugar. Leave in a warm place until frothy.

Place the flours, salt and butter in the bowl, and mix for a few seconds, using the double-bladed chopping knife. Pour the yeast liquid through the feed tube and mix to form a dough. Turn onto a floured board and knead for 1 minute. Cover and leave in a warm place to rise until doubled in size – about 1 hour. Knead again (this second kneading is known as 'knocking back') and shape into a round. Place on a greased baking tray and cut a cross on top of the dough. Cover and prove for 30 minutes in a warm place. Brush with a little salt water and sprinkle with cracked wheat. Bake in a hot oven (220 C, 425 F, gas 7) for 20-30 minutes.

Different Ways to Shape Bread
Bread Plait Divide the knocked-back dough into three equal portions. Roll each into a long thin piece and pinch these together at one end. Plait the pieces neatly on a greased baking tray, then leave to prove until doubled in size and bake as above.
Cottage Loaf Divide the knocked-back dough into two portions, one smaller than the other. Place the larger piece of dough on a greased baking tray and top with the smaller ball of dough. Make an indentation, using your thumb or two fingers, right down the middle of the loaf. Prove and bake as above.

From the top: Granary Loaf, Devil's Food Cake (page 69) and Wholemeal Drop Scones (overleaf)

WHOLEMEAL DROP SCONES

MAKES ABOUT 30

175 g/6 oz strong plain flour
175 g/6 oz plain wholemeal flour
15 g/½ oz fresh yeast
300 ml/½ pint warm water
200 ml/7 fl oz milk
¼ teaspoon salt
½ teaspoon bicarbonate of soda

Mix the flours and pour half into a mixing bowl. Mix the yeast with the water until well combined. Pour into the centre of the flour and leave until frothy.

Place in the bowl and gradually mix in the remaining flour, using the double-bladed chopping knife. Pour the milk onto the dough through the feed tube and mix until the batter is smooth. Lastly, add the salt and bicarbonate of soda. Place spoonfuls of the yeast batter on a greased griddle or frying pan and cook over a low heat. When bubbles appear on the surface turn over and cook on the other side. Serve hot with butter.

SPICED OATIES

MAKES 14-16

175 g/6 oz plain flour
75 g/3 oz butter
50 g/2 oz medium oatmeal
50 g/2 oz chopped mixed nuts
25 g/1 oz demerara sugar
¼ teaspoon allspice
4 tablespoons milk
1 egg yolk
demerara sugar to sprinkle

Mix the flour and butter, using the double-bladed chopping knife, until the mixture resembles fine breadcrumbs. Transfer to a mixing bowl and stir in the oatmeal, nuts, sugar and allspice. Mix the milk and egg yolk and make a well in the centre of the flour mixture. Stir in the liquid gradually to form a biscuit dough. Knead lightly on a floured surface until smooth. Roll out to 3 mm/⅛ in thick and cut out 6-cm/2½-in rounds. Arrange on greased baking trays and bake in a moderately hot oven (200 C, 400 F, gas 6) for 10-15 minutes. Sprinkle the biscuits with sugar while hot and leave to cool on racks.

PEACH AND ORANGE TEABREAD

MAKES 1 (1-kg/2-lb) LOAF

100 g/4 oz dried peaches, soaked overnight
100 g/4 oz glacé cherries
grated rind and juice of 2 small oranges
50 g/2 oz butter
225 g/8 oz self-raising flour
75 g/3 oz soft brown sugar
100 g/4 oz raisins
2 eggs
1-2 tablespoons milk

Drain the peaches and chop with the cherries, using the double-bladed chopping knife. Simmer the chopped fruit in the orange juice for 5 minutes.

Using the double-bladed chopping knife, mix the butter into the flour. Add the remaining ingredients and mix well. Place in a greased 1-kg/2-lb loaf tin. Bake in a moderate oven (180 C, 350 F, gas 4) for 1-1¼ hours. Slice and spread with butter.

CHERRY GÂTEAU

SERVES 6-8

175 g/6 oz butter
175 g/6 oz castor sugar
3 eggs
165 g/5½ oz self-raising flour
15 g/½ oz cocoa powder, sieved
Filling:
1 (142-ml/5-fl oz) carton black cherry yogurt
1 (425-g/15-oz) can black cherries, drained
150 ml/¼ pint double cream

Cream the butter and sugar together until light and fluffy, using the double-bladed chopping knife. Add the eggs one at a time, adding a little of the flour with each egg after the first. Mix well between each addition. Add the remaining flour and cocoa and mix for a few seconds only. If the flour has not been completely incorporated, use a spatula to fold it in. Grease and base line two (20-cm/8-in) sandwich tins. Bake in the centre of a moderate oven (160 C, 325 F, gas 3) for 30-40 minutes.

Turn out and cool on a wire tray. When cool, sandwich the cakes together with the yogurt and half the canned cherries. Whip the cream and spread a little over the top of the gâteau. Pipe the remaining cream around the edge and fill the centre with the remaining cherries.

Note If liked the gâteau can be sprinkled with some of the canned cherry juice before assembling.

FLORENTINES

MAKES 18

25 g/1 oz walnuts
25 g/1 oz raisins
50 g/2 oz glacé cherries
50 g/2 oz demerara sugar
1 tablespoon golden syrup
50 g/2 oz butter
40 g/1½ oz plain flour
25 g/1 oz mixed cut peel
75 g/3 oz chocolate, melted

Using the double-bladed chopping knife, finely chop the walnuts, raisins and glacé cherries.

Melt the sugar, syrup and butter together, remove from the heat and add all the remaining ingredients except the chocolate. Place teaspoonfuls of the mixture well apart on greased baking trays. Bake in a moderate oven (180 C, 350 F, gas 4) for 8-10 minutes. Remove carefully with a palette knife and allow to cool.

Spread one side of each florentine with melted chocolate and mark a design on each, using a fork.

ALMOND SHORTBREAD

MAKES 14 FINGERS

100 g/4 oz plain flour
50 g/2 oz rice flour
50 g/2 oz ground almonds
100 g/4 oz butter
75 g/3 oz sugar
1 egg yolk
2 tablespoons milk
few drops of almond essence
castor sugar to sprinkle

Mix the flour, rice flour, ground almonds and butter together, using the double-bladed chopping knife, until the mixture resembles fine breadcrumbs. Add the remaining ingredients and mix into a dough. Place in an 18-cm/7-in square shallow tin, pressing down until smooth. Prick all over with a fork. Bake in a moderate oven (180 C, 350 F, gas 4) for 50-60 minutes. Mark into fingers while hot and sprinkle with sugar.

DEVIL'S FOOD CAKE

S E R V E S 8 - 1 0

175 g/6 oz soft margarine
175 g/6 oz golden syrup
175 g/6 oz castor sugar
50 g/2 oz ground almonds
175 g/6 oz plain flour
50 g/2 oz cocoa powder
175 ml/6 fl oz milk
2 eggs
100 g/4 oz toasted flaked almonds to decorate
Icing:
1 tablespoon cocoa powder
2 tablespoons hot water
75 g/3 oz butter
225 g/8 oz icing sugar

Place the margarine, syrup and dry ingredients in the bowl and mix, using the double-bladed chopping knife, until the fat is incorporated. Beat the milk and eggs together and add through the feed tube until well combined. Pour the mixture into two greased and lined 20-cm/8-in sandwich tins. Bake in a cool oven (150C, 300F, gas 2) for 50-55 minutes. Turn out and cool on a wire rack.

For the icing, mix together the cocoa and hot water, then combine all the ingredients, using the double-bladed chopping knife. Use the icing to sandwich the two layers together and to spread over the top and sides of the cake, piping decoratively if desired. Press flaked almonds around the sides.

QUICK ORANGE CAKE

S E R V E S 8 - 1 0

100 g/4 oz soft margarine
100 g/4 oz castor sugar
grated rind of 1 orange
100 g/4 oz self-raising flour
½ teaspoon baking powder
2 eggs
Filling:
150 ml/¼ pint double cream
2 tablespoons icing sugar
grated rind and juice of 1 orange
4 tablespoons orange marmalade
Decoration:
225 g/8 oz icing sugar
2-3 tablespoons orange juice
1 orange, sliced

Place the margarine, sugar, orange rind and dry ingredients in the bowl with the eggs. Mix using the double-bladed chopping knife or plastic blade until smooth and soft. Be careful not to overmix. Divide between two greased and bottom-lined 20-cm/8-in sandwich tins. Bake in a moderate oven (180C, 350F, gas 4) for 25-30 minutes. Turn out and cool on a wire rack.

For the filling, whip the cream with the icing sugar, orange rind and juice. Spread one cooled cake with marmalade and most of the cream, then place the second cake on top.

For the icing, sieve the icing sugar into a bowl and beat in the orange juice. Spread this on top of the cake. Add the orange slices as shown in the picture then pipe or spoon small dots of the reserved cream between them.

Quick Orange Cake

Sauces

This chapter offers a variety of recipes which may be used to enhance the flavour of meat, fish, vegetable and pasta dishes, making simple foods into something special. There is nothing to compare with the flavour of freshly made sauces such as mint, apple and cranberry, which can be made in minutes. Espagnole, a sauce which can be used as a basis for making other classic sauces, is useful to make in bulk and freeze for use later. Sauces can be made with complete confidence using the food processor, producing successful results every time.

BASIC MAYONNAISE

MAKES 300ml / ½ pint

liquidizer.

1 egg (wann)
1 teaspoon castor sugar
pinch of mustard powder
salt and freshly ground black pepper
300 ml/½ pint oil (wann)
1 teaspoon wine vinegar

Place the egg, sugar, mustard and seasoning in the bowl and mix for a few seconds using the double-bladed chopping knife. With the motor switched on, pour the oil through the feed tube in a slow trickle. The mayonnaise will thicken slowly. Mix in the vinegar at the end.

Variations

Avocado Mayonnaise Peel an avocado and remove the stone. Add the flesh to the egg and seasonings and continue as above.

Garlic Mayonnaise Add a crushed clove of garlic to the egg and seasonings and continue as above.

Green Mayonnaise Leave the mayonnaise in the bowl and add a handful of washed watercress leaves. Using the double-bladed chopping knife, mix until the watercress is very finely chopped.

Cucumber Mayonnaise Peel a quarter of a cucumber and place in the feed tube. Grate, using the grating disc. Drain well and stir into the prepared mayonnaise with a few chopped chives.

Tartare Sauce Finely chop 2 gherkins, 1 spring onion and 2 tablespoons capers, using the double-bladed chopping knife. Stir into the prepared mayonnaise.

REMOULADE SAUCE

MAKES 300ml / ½ pint

300 ml/½ pint Basic mayonnaise (see page 70)
4 anchovy fillets
1 teaspoon French mustard
few sprigs parsley
1 teaspoon capers
1 gherkin
few sprigs fresh tarragon

First make the mayonnaise. Chop the remaining ingredients together, using the double-bladed chopping knife. Add the mayonnaise to the chopped ingredients and mix quickly for a few seconds until well combined. Serve with cold meat, poultry and shellfish.

WATERCRESS DRESSING

MAKES 150ml / 57 pint

2 bunches watercress
150 ml/¼ pint double cream
salt and freshly ground black pepper
few drops lemon juice

Trim the watercress, removing any tough stems. Place in a saucepan with a little water and bring to the boil. Simmer for 5-8 minutes. Drain well and chop finely, using the double-bladed chopping knife.

Bring the cream to the boil and stir in the finely chopped watercress. Season to taste and add a few drops of lemon juice. Serve with salmon.

BREAD SAUCE

MAKES 300ml / ½ pint

1 onion
6 cloves
300 ml/½ pint milk
2 slices white bread
25 g/1 oz butter
salt and freshly ground black pepper

Peel the onion and stud with the cloves. Place the milk in a saucepan with the onion. Bring to the boil and simmer gently for 10 minutes.

Remove the crusts and make the bread into breadcrumbs, using the double-bladed chopping knife.

Remove the onion from the milk, stir in the breadcrumbs and infuse for 30 minutes. Add the butter and reheat, stirring all the time. Season to taste.

Hollandaise Sauce

HOLLANDAISE SAUCE

MAKES 150ml / ¼ pint

3 egg yolks
3 tablespoons boiling water
1 tablespoon wine vinegar
1 tablespoon lemon juice
100 g/4 oz butter, melted

Place the yolks and boiling water in the bowl and mix well, using the double-bladed chopping knife. Add the vinegar and lemon juice and mix again. Slowly pour the melted butter through the feed tube, with the motor running. Transfer the sauce to a small bowl and place over a saucepan of hot water. Stir continuously until thick. Serve immediately.

ONION SAUCE

MAKES 300ml / ½ pint

2 onions
25 g/1 oz plain flour
25 g/1 oz butter
300 ml/½ pint milk
salt and freshly ground black pepper
2 tablespoons single cream

Peel the onions and slice thinly, using the slicing disc. Cook in boiling water for 10 minutes, then drain.

Place the flour, butter and milk in a saucepan and bring to the boil whisking all the time. Season and add the drained onions and cream. This sauce goes well with lamb.

Variation
Cheese Sauce Omit the onions from the above recipe. Grate 100 g/4 oz matured Cheddar cheese, using the grating disc, and add it to the other ingredients in the saucepan. Whisk and cook as in the above recipe.

SPICY TOMATO SAUCE

MAKES 300ml / ½ pint

1 onion
2 carrots
2 sticks celery
2 rashers bacon, rinds removed
25 g/1 oz butter
1 tablespoon oil
25 g/1 oz plain flour
1 (425-g/15-oz) can tomatoes
3 tablespoons tomato purée
¼ teaspoon ground mace
freshly grated nutmeg
salt and freshly ground black pepper
few sprigs parsley
sprig fresh basil
150 ml/¼ pint stock
sugar to taste

Peel and clean the vegetables and chop roughly with the bacon, using the double-bladed chopping knife. Melt the butter and oil and sauté the chopped vegetables and bacon. Stir in the flour and cook for 1 minute. Add the remaining ingredients and bring to the boil. Cover and simmer for 45 minutes.

Purée the sauce until smooth, using the double-bladed chopping knife. Adjust the seasoning if necessary.

ESPAGNOLE SAUCE

MAKES 300ml / ½ pint

1 onion
1 stick celery
2 small carrots
4 mushrooms
2 rashers bacon, rinds removed
2 tablespoons oil
25 g/1 oz plain flour
450 ml/¾ pint stock
2 tablespoons tomato purée
salt and freshly ground black pepper
3 tablespoons chopped parsley
1 bay leaf

Peel and clean the vegetables and chop roughly with the bacon, using the double-bladed chopping knife. Heat the oil and sauté the vegetables until golden. Stir in the flour and cook for a few minutes until golden brown. Gradually stir in the stock and the remaining ingredients. Bring to the boil, cover and simmer for 45-60 minutes.

Remove the bay leaf and purée the sauce until smooth, using the double-bladed chopping knife. If preferred, the sauce can be sieved before serving. Serve with meat dishes.

FRESH MINT SAUCE

MAKES ABOUT 150ml / ¼ pint

large bunch fresh mint leaves
2 tablespoons boiling water
2 tablespoons sugar
2-3 tablespoons wine vinegar

Trim the mint, removing the stalks. Chop finely, using the double-blased chopping knife. Place the chopped mint in a small basin and pour over the boiling water and sugar. Stir well and leave until cold. Add the vinegar and serve.

CRANBERRY SAUCE

MAKES 300ml / ½ pint

150 ml/¼ pint water
175 g/6 oz sugar
225 g/8 oz cranberries
lemon juice, to taste

Dissolve the sugar and water over a low heat. Bring to the boil and add the cranberries. Cover and simmer until the fruit is soft: 8-10 minutes. Cool and then mix to a purée, using the double-bladed chopping knife. Add lemon juice to taste.

APPLE SAUCE

MAKES 300ml / ½ pint

450 g/1 lb cooking apples
2-3 tablespoons water
sugar, to taste
15 g/½ oz butter

Peel, core and slice the apples and place in a saucepan with the water. Cook until the apple becomes soft. Allow to cool then mix to a purée with the sugar and butter, using the double-bladed chopping knife.

ITALIAN SAUCE

MAKES 150ml / ¼ pint

few sprigs fresh basil or parsley
50 g/2 oz Parmesan cheese, broken into chunks
3-4 tablespoons peanut or olive oil
25 g/1 oz walnuts
1 clove garlic
salt and freshly ground black pepper

Finely chop the herbs and Parmesan, using the double-bladed chopping knife, until a paste is formed – about 1-2 minutes. Pour the oil slowly through the feed tube and mix until well combined. Add the nuts, garlic and seasoning and mix to a soft paste.

Use as a topping for soups or toss with hot cooked pasta.

Italian Sauce

PEANUT BUTTER SPREAD
MAKES 175 g / 6 oz

100 g/4 oz salted peanuts
50 g/2 oz butter
salt

Finely chop the peanuts, using the double-bladed chopping knife. Add the butter and mix to form a smooth paste, using the double-bladed chopping knife. Add salt to taste.
  Store in the refrigerator and use as required.

HERB BUTTER
MAKES 100 g / 4 oz

few sprigs of fresh herbs
100 g/4 oz butter
salt and freshly ground black pepper

Chop the herbs finely, using the double-bladed chopping knife. Mix the herbs, butter and seasoning together thoroughly, using the double-bladed chopping knife. Serve with steak or other grilled meat.

Herb Bread Cut a French loaf three-quarters through into slices, leaving all the pieces attached underneath. Spread herb butter generously between each slice, wrap the loaf in foil and bake in a moderately hot oven (200 C, 400 F, gas 6) for 20 minutes. Separate the slices and serve immediately. (Illustrated on page 23)

CHEDDAR CHEESE SPREAD
MAKES 175 g / 6 oz

100 g/4 oz Cheddar cheese
50 g/2 oz butter
salt and freshly ground black pepper
pinch of mustard powder

Grate the cheese finely, using the grating disc. Place in the bowl with the butter, seasonings and mustard and mix thoroughly, using the double-bladed chopping knife. Store in the refrigerator.

Variations
Add one of the following to the basic cheese spread mixtures:
25 g/1 oz chopped nuts
1 tablespoon mango chutney
1 hard-boiled egg, finely chopped
1 tablespoon chopped parsley
½ teaspoon curry paste

Peanut Butter Spread and Spiced Oaties (page 66)

Index